Life in VICTORIAN Times

Work & Industry

Neil Morris

First published in the UK in 1999 by
Belitha Press Limited, London House,
Great Eastern Wharf, Parkgate Road,
London SW11 4NQ

ISBN 1 85561 891 5

British Library Cataloguing in Publication Data for this book is available from the British Library.

Series editor: Honor Head
Series designer: Jamie Asher
Picture researcher: Diana Morris
Consultant: Sallie Purkis

Printed in Singapore

Picture credits

Hulton Getty Picture Collection: front cover bl, 4t, 4b, 5t, 5b, 8, 9t, 9b, 11t, 11b, 12, 13t, 15b, 16, 17t, 18, 20, 21c, 22, 23c, 24b, 25t ,29tl, 29tr, 29b.

Public Record Office: front cover top and br, back cover, 1, 3, 6, 7t, 7b, 8,10, 13c, 13b,14, 15t, 17c, 17b, 19t, 19 b, 21t, 21b, 23t, 23b, 24t, 25b, 26, 27t, 27c, 27b, 28, 29tr.

Words in **bold** are in the glossary on pages 30 and 31.

ANDREW

CONTENTS

INTRODUCTION

Trade and industry changed dramatically during the Victorian period. The invention of new machines and the growth of factories affected the working lives of most people. Steam power meant that many jobs could now be done by machines, and these needed workers to keep them running. Coal was essential to help make the steam which powered the machines, so the coal mining industry grew. Huge **industrial** towns grew around the factories which made more goods for sale at home and abroad.

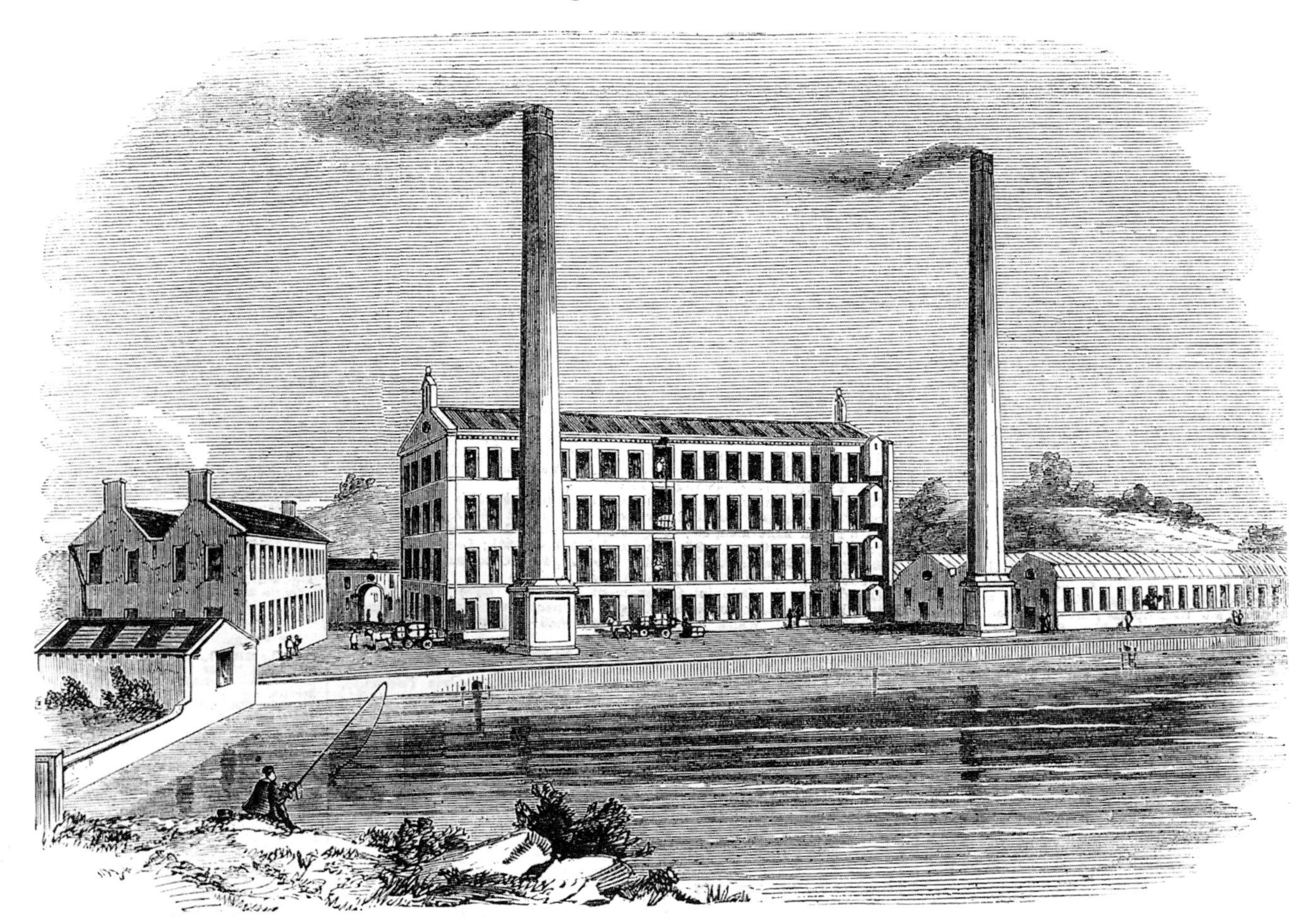

We use the word Victorian to describe the time when Queen Victoria was on the British throne. Born in 1819, Victoria was the only child of Edward, the fourth son of King George III, and Victoria Maria Louisa, the daughter of a German duke. She became queen in 1837, and three years later married Albert, a German prince. They had nine children before Albert died in 1861. Victoria ruled for almost 64 years, longer than any other British monarch. She died in 1901, at the age of 81.

To begin with conditions in the factories were poor, and the new machines were often not very safe. Working hours were long and the factory owners **exploited** their workers, especially women and children. But people were desperate for work. Those without jobs were not well looked after, and many were forced into dreadful **workhouses.**

For most ordinary people working conditions had improved by the end of the Victorian period. Farmworkers had machines to help them. In the factories, new laws and **trade unions** were helping to improve conditions, and people generally had a bit more money to spend. New inventions such as the **telegraph** and the typewriter created different kinds of jobs. The world of work was very different as people headed towards the new century.

IN THE FACTORY

Steam-powered machines meant that more goods could be made and much faster than when they were made by hand. When manufacturers realized this, they put their machines into huge factories, so that all the work could be done in one place. Many Victorian factories were built near coal mines, because coal was burned to make the steam that powered the machines.

Industrial towns grew very quickly in the nineteenth century as people moved to factory areas to look for work. For example, in 1800, 75 000 lived in Manchester. By 1850, more than 300 000 people lived there. Factory workers had no rights and had to work long hours in dreadful conditions for low pay.

The main task for most factory workers was to make sure that the machines kept running properly. Because the machines were difficult and expensive to start up, factory owners wanted to keep them going all the time. This meant that some workers had to work all night. During the day, workers would often have to stay at their machine for up to 12 hours at a time, with just a few short breaks.

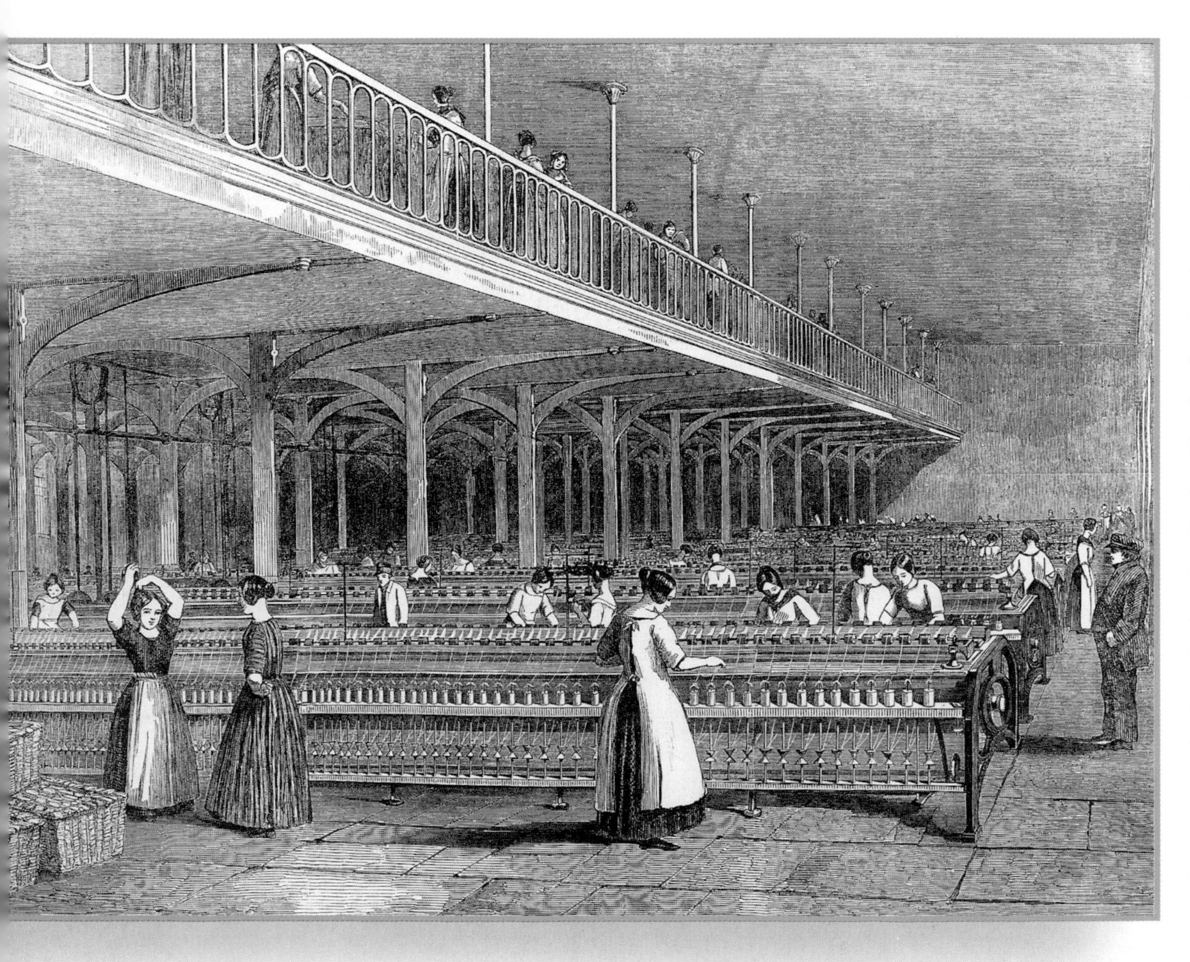

◄ *Before the growth of factories, cloth was made at home by the women and children. When textile mills began to open, like this one near Bolton, in Lancashire, women and children were employed to do the spinning and weaving and the men would* **oversee** *the work. Although the women worked as hard as the men, they were paid only half a man's wage. This mill produced fine thread for making into lace.*

▲ *Workers who used their hands had to do very repetitive work. They were not allowed to talk to each other or take breaks when they wanted. Overseers made sure that they worked as fast as they could. Workers were fined if they arrived late or if they broke a tool by accident. This illustration shows young women grinding and shaping steel pens in a Birmingham factory in 1851. By this time people used pens with steel* ***nibs*** *for writing rather than goose* ***quills****, but the nibs still needed to be dipped in ink. The factory produced more than 262 million pens a year. The women earned between five and seven shillings (25p to 35p) a week.*

▼ *This 1885 advertisement for a factory in Sheffield, Yorkshire, shows the different processes needed for electroplating. This process coated steel with silver or other metals. The city of Sheffield became Britain's main centre of steel production, and is still world-famous for cutlery today.*

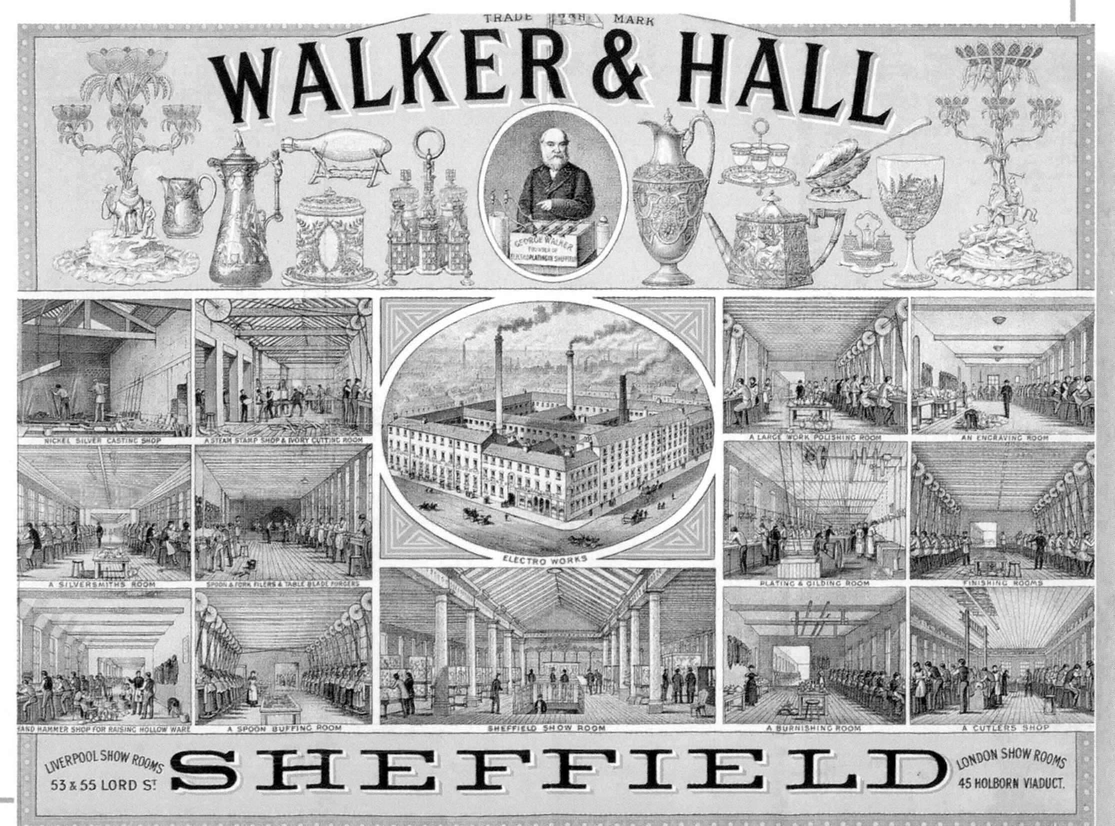

HOMEWORKERS

Many goods were produced in large quantities in huge factories in Victorian times. But some people still worked in a more traditional way, making things at home.

Cottage industries had existed for a long time in country areas, and they continued in places where there was no nearby town. Working life was hard for homeworkers. Most were poorly paid for piecework, in other words for the amount that they produced, however long it took them. Others took the risk of making things and then trying to sell them, in the local markets for example.

Before the end of the nineteenth century new laws helped to improve the quality of life for factory workers, but they did little for homeworkers. By the end of the Victorian age, people who worked in factories had better pay and working conditions than those who worked at home.

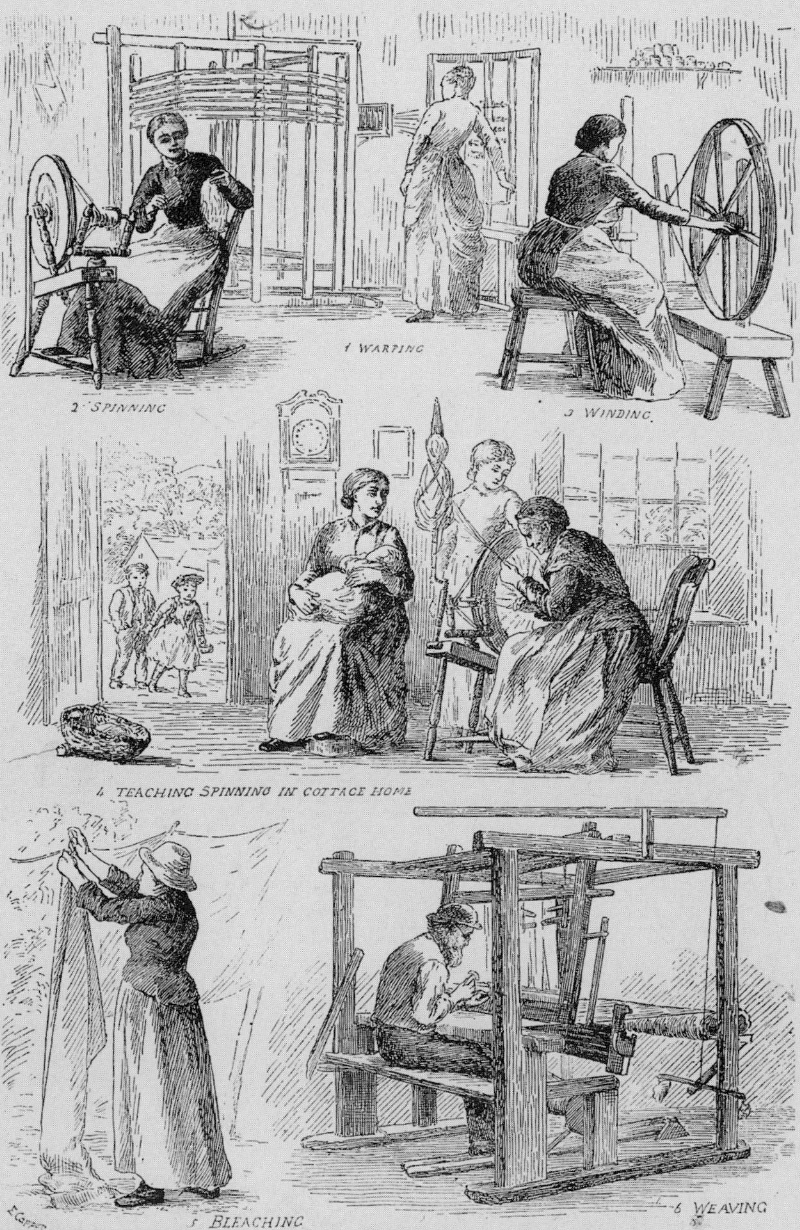

► *Spinning and weaving were traditional cottage industries, and they continued to be so despite the rise of steam-powered factories. In this series of drawings, a journal of 1886 described what it called 'women's industries' in north-west England. At home, power was provided by human muscles, through foot-operated* ***treadles****. As with many traditional crafts, the techniques were passed down in families from generation to generation. As illustrated in the middle picture, Victorian working-class women had the difficult task of bringing up and looking after children as well as trying to work, just as many women do today. During the nineteenth century many younger people began to move away from their homes in the country to search for work in the growing towns.*

◄ *A mother and daughter make cards and small gifts for St Valentine's Day, in 1875. They were paid very little for each item made and worked solidly during most of the daylight hours. Valentines became very popular in the middle of the nineteenth century, when penny postage, pillar boxes and envelopes were introduced. Valentine cards were mostly hand-painted, and homeworkers decorated them with dried flowers, feathers and tassels.*

▼ *This photograph shows a woman preparing wool in the Shetland Islands. The people who lived on these islands off the Scottish mainland have traditionally reared sheep and fished. Shetland wool is considered to be very high quality and is still famous today. The woman in the photograph is 'carding', or untangling wool fibres to make them ready for spinning into woollen* ***yarn.***

THE WORKHOUSE

A new Poor Law was passed in 1834, three years before Victoria became queen. Many rich people and politicians felt that too much money was being paid out to help **paupers** and poor people. Under the new law, the poor would have to work for their **welfare**, and many new workhouses were built.

Workhouses were meant to be unpleasant places, so that people would try very hard to avoid them. Well-off Victorians believed that this was for poor peoples' own good. But many of the country's poor lived in areas where work was hard to find outside the workhouses so they were unable to help themselves.

Because workhouses were so hated, many able-bodied poor chose to take their chances outside. The workhouses became places for the old, the very young, the sick and the mentally ill. They continued throughout the nineteenth century, and we look back on them now as a symbol of hard-hearted, even cruel, Victorian attitudes.

◄ *This 1892 poster shows an alternative approach to helping the poor. The Church of England could afford to offer homes to 'waifs and strays' – homeless and neglected children – by encouraging them to make and sell stockings. In this way a poor child who lived on the streets could be given work and shelter. Local churches and other charity organizations also ran soup kitchens and offered alternatives to the dreaded workhouse.*

▲ *In the workhouse, men, women and children had to eat separately. This picture shows women's dinner time at St Pancras workhouse, London, in 1895. At one time St Pancras had up to 2000* ***inmates****, and half of them were old people who were not well enough to work. Workhouse food was very dull, and not at all* ***nutritious****. Inmates were often fed on gruel, a thin porridge of oatmeal boiled in water. Generally no talking was allowed at meal times. Those who broke the rules were fed bread and water.*

▼ *This illustration shows the Andover Union workhouse, in Hampshire. Under the new Poor Law, 20 or 30 local* ***parishes*** *had to join together to form a union. Each union built one workhouse, which had separate* ***dormitories*** *and exercise yards for men and women. This meant that children were separated from parents, and brothers from sisters. Everyone had to wear a plain uniform, so it is easy to see why many inmates thought of the place as a prison. The master of Andover ran his workhouse so strictly that there was an official investigation in 1846. It found that some of the inmates were so hungry that they ate food meant for pigs and chickens.*

CHILD LABOUR

One of the worst aspects of working life in Victorian Britain was that children were sent out to work from a very young age. Many parents needed the extra money that children could earn, though they were paid much less than adults. Working-class children had always been expected to work, and this was not viewed with the horror it is today. **Orphans** were even sold as apprentices to mill owners.

Children could do some jobs better than adults because of their size. Small climbing boys worked for chimney sweeps, clambering up the long, twisting chimneys of big houses to clear away the soot from coal fires. Sweeps thought that the best age for teaching boys to climb was about six, though after 1844 children could not officially start work until they were eight. Many climbing boys were crippled or killed, and in 1875 a law finally put a stop to the practice. Small children were also used for cleaning out machinery, for example to remove fluff from under **looms**. They had to do this while the machines were running, so it was very dangerous work.

▼ *In early Victorian times very young children worked in coal mines. Tiny boys and girls opened and closed shaft doors, and older, stronger children filled and pushed coal trucks. They did this for up to 12 hours a day. In 1842 a law stated that no children under the age of ten and no females could work underground.*

◄ *This young girl is helping a craftsman to print on to a fabric called* ***calico****, in the 1840s. The craftsman is using a block to transfer the inked design on to the fabric. Children who learned a trade in this way found it much easier to find work when they were older. At this time many children never went to school at all.*

► *A boy helps to make wooden clock-cases in an east London workshop in the 1850s. As well as doing some woodworking, he probably also ran errands and did odd jobs. Workshops such as this used English oak, but they also had to* ***import*** *some of the wood they needed, such as mahogany.*

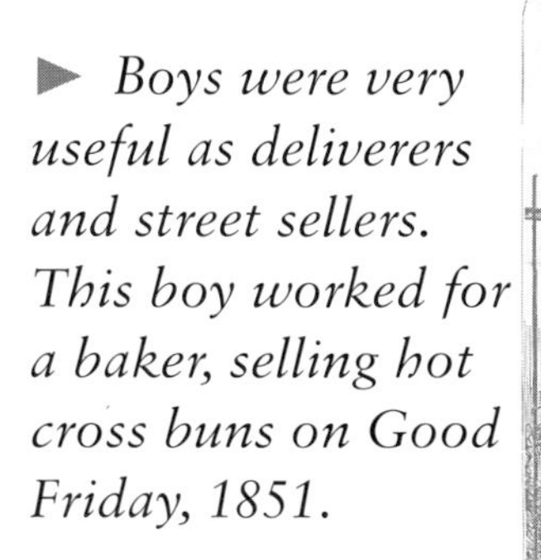

► *Boys were very useful as deliverers and street sellers. This boy worked for a baker, selling hot cross buns on Good Friday, 1851.*

STEAM POWER

More than 50 years before the start of Victoria's reign, the Scotsman James Watt invented a way of using steam engines to drive machines. In his **rotary engine**, coal was burned to heat water and turn it to steam; the steam drove a series of **cogs** which turned a driving belt, which could be used for all sorts of purposes.

Factory owners, especially those manufacturing cotton and textiles, liked steam-powered machines. They saved time and money. At the very beginning of Victorian times, a mill owner calculated that a single steam engine had the power of 880 men and could drive 50 000 **spindles** in a spinning machine. A steam engine needed 750 workers to keep it running, which seems a lot, but it could produce as much yarn as 200 000 workers could make by hand.

Steam-powered machines began to turn out more goods than ever before. This meant that the coal industry was vitally important. Vast amounts of coal were needed to make the steel which was used for the machines, as well as to provide fuel for the steam engines which powered the machines.

► *Steam was used to power printing presses. This illustration shows steam-powered machines printing copies of* The Illustrated London News. *There are two machines, one for printing one side of the paper, and another for printing the reverse. Paper was fed into the rollers by hand. The rollers moved the paper across the inking-table below. The machines could print 2000 sheets an hour. Both machines were run by a single six-**horsepower** steam engine.*

◄ *Steam was used to run factory machines throughout the Victorian period. By the end of the century manufacturers were looking for ways to make steam even more efficient. This poster of 1900 shows how a factory in Wakefield, Yorkshire, re-used waste gases to heat water. This was purely to save money. The Victorians had little idea about the effects of* ***pollution****, and people thought that coal was an everlasting source of energy.*

► *James Nasmyth (1808-90), a Scottish engineer, invented the steam hammer in 1839. This illustration shows a large steam hammer at work in an iron* ***foundry*** *around 1850. The hammer was used to shape large pieces of metal and to* ***forge*** *parts for railways and steamships. Steam was used to raise the heavy hammer head, which then dropped down by its own weight. Extra steam could be used to force the hammer down even faster.*

THE GREAT EXHIBITION

The Great Exhibition was held in London in 1851. It displayed more than 100 000 industrial exhibits from all over the world, but most were British. This was an opportunity to show that Great Britain was the 'workshop of the world' and to win new orders both at home and abroad.

Many people think that the idea for the exhibition was thought up by Prince Albert, Queen Victoria's husband. But it was probably originally the idea of Henry Cole, a designer and writer who was a member of the Society for the Encouragement of Arts, Manufactures and Commerce. Prince Albert was president of the society, and he certainly supported the idea of the exhibition.

Prince Albert agreed that the exhibition could be held in Hyde Park, and the planning committee – headed by the prince – held a competition for the best design. This was won by the architect Joseph Paxton, who came up with an idea rather like a giant greenhouse – a Crystal Palace. The exhibition was a great success. It ran for 20 weeks and had more than six million visitors.

◄ *Crystal Palace was over 600 metres long and 120 metres wide. The iron frame of the building supported nearly 300 000 panes of glass, which were fitted by 80 workmen. Altogether 2000 people worked on the building, which was finished just 15 months after it was decided to hold the exhibition. It was built so quickly because the parts were all a standard size, and easily put together. Two years later, the building was taken down and moved to Sydenham, in Kent. The Crystal Palace was destroyed by fire in 1936.*

▲ *Queen Victoria opened the exhibition on 1 May, 1851. Here, she is seated in front of one of the three elm trees that were left growing inside the glasshouse. She was very excited by the exhibition, and wrote in her diary: 'The tremendous cheers, the joy on every face, and all due to my husband, the author of this 'Peace Festival' which united the industry and art of all nations.' The queen enjoyed herself so much that she went to the exhibition almost every day for the first three months, visiting all the exhibits.*

▲ *Cotton machines were on display in the Machinery Department of the exhibition. The Crystal Palace had a special boiler room with steam engines to run the machinery.*

► *The Canadian Court showed sledges and a trading canoe made of bark. The Victorians were very proud of their Canadian colonies. Between 1815 and 1850, almost a million people had sailed from Britain to settle in Canada.*

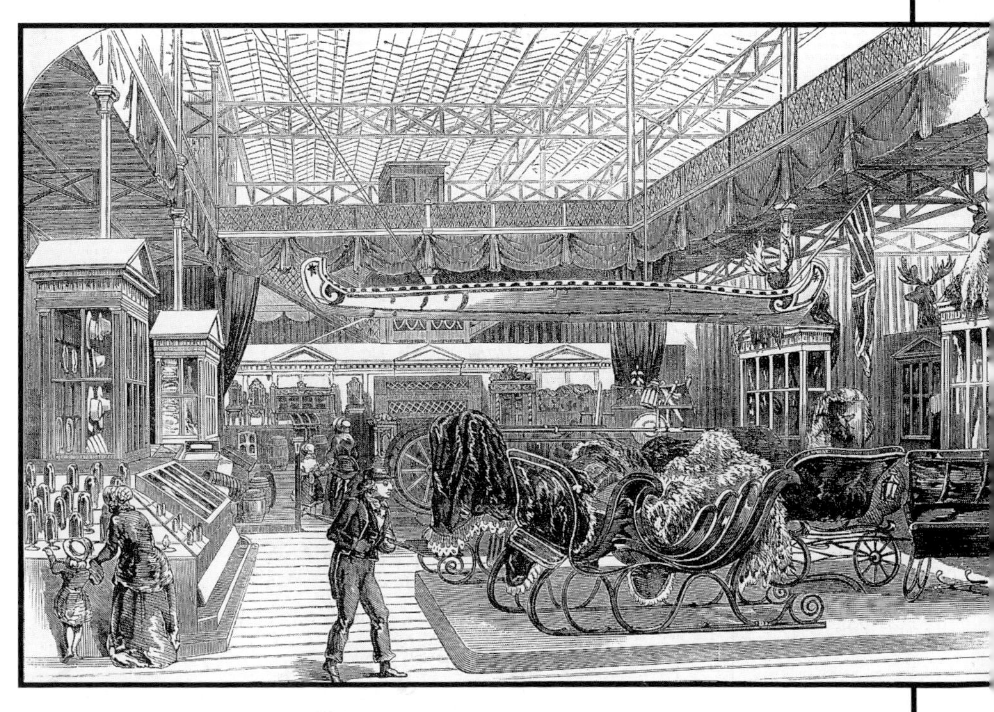

IRON AND STEEL

Iron production was important throughout Victorian times. In British ironworks, pig-iron – the crude form of the metal that is made in a smelting furnace – was turned into wrought iron. This tougher form of iron was hammered, rolled and used in the first half of the nineteenth century to make machines, railway tracks, ships and bridges. By 1850 Britain made half the world's pig-iron and was shipping huge quantities to other countries. This helped pay for the goods Britain needed to import.

Cast iron was used to make the frame for the Great Exhibition's Crystal Palace. At this time steel was hardly used because it was very expensive to make. Four years later, the English inventor, Henry Bessemer, found a way of making cheap steel, which was harder and stronger than iron. His new process cut the price of steel by half, and the world's first steel railway tracks were laid on the London and North Western Railway in 1862.

By 1871 Britain produced 40 per cent of the world's steel. British steel was used for great feats of Victorian engineering, such as the Forth Bridge in Scotland, which opened in 1890.

► *Henry Bessemer (1813-98)* ***patented*** *his method of making steel – called the Bessemer process – in 1855. In the process, pig-iron was produced first. Then this passed into a furnace called a converter (in the foreground) where air was blown through the molten iron. This burned out most of the iron's impurities, giving off a spectacular shower of sparks. Some Bessemer converters are still used today. Altogether Bessemer patented 114 inventions. One of the most profitable was a method of making gold paint.*

▲ *Working with iron was hard, hot and very dangerous. These men are casting a huge cylinder, 2.4 metres in diameter, at an ironworks in east London, in 1863. It took 12 men two months to prepare the moulds for the casting. The cylinder was part of a steam engine for a new steamship for the Peninsular and Oriental Steam Navigation Company (P&O).*

► *Some of the Victorian tools, utensils and other goods that were made from iron and steel are shown in this illustration from 1884. The Victorians were great inventors, engineers and craftsmen, and the design of many of these goods has come back into fashion over a hundred years later. Before the end of the nineteenth century, both the USA and Germany began to produce more steel than Britain.*

DOMESTIC SERVICE

Throughout Victorian times, domestic service was a great source of employment for many people. In 1850 there were more than a million household servants in Britain, which made them one of the largest working groups in the country. Twenty years later, more than a third of all British girls between the ages of 12 and 20 were in domestic service.

Rich people employed many male and female servants in their huge town and country homes. The Duke of Bedford, for example, had 300 servants. Middle-class families also had servants. Even some working-class people had a maid, though she was usually a young relative who worked just for her board and lodging.

Most Victorian servants were not paid very well, but they had the advantage of being well fed and given clothing and shelter. This meant a great deal to young people, especially uneducated girls from poor families, who would otherwise have found it difficult to find a job and support themselves.

◀ *This group photograph shows the servants in front of Erddig Hall, near Wrexham in north Wales, in 1852. The man in the middle of the front row is opening a bottle of wine. He was the household's* ***butler****, who was in charge of all the other male servants as well as the wine cellar. In big country houses many men were needed to look after the buildings, coaches, horses and gardens. The gardener at the back of the group is holding a watering can.* ***Footmen*** *in uniform, such as the young man on the left, opened doors, helped serve meals and carried messages. Footmen were usually tall, since their employers wanted them to look as impressive as possible to their visitors.*

◄ *In this 1893 advertisement, the lady of the house is served by her maid. In a large household, all the female staff reported to a* ***housekeeper****, who held a high rank like a butler. The lady's children were looked after by a* ***nanny****, and there was usually a* ***governess*** *to teach the children at home.*

► *A group of Victorian maidservants help with the cooking. The photograph seems very posed. Perhaps the lady of the house wanted a picture of the maids for a family album.*

◄ *A maid does the ironing in 1899. She is using a flat iron, which was a solid piece of smooth, heavy metal that had to be heated on the fire. Maids heated several flat irons at once. The first electric iron appeared in France in 1880, but electric kitchen utensils were not in general use until much later. Washing and cleaning was all done by hand, which meant plenty of hard work for the servants.*

BETTER CONDITIONS

Conditions for workers, especially those in factories, gradually improved throughout the nineteenth century. Most employers thought that their workers should consider themselves lucky to have jobs, so they did little to improve working conditions. But many new laws were passed which forced factory owners and others to change their ways.

The Factory Act of 1847 changed the law so that women and children under the age of 18 could work only ten hours a day. Twenty years later, another Factory Act reduced all factory workers to a 10-hour day. Many of these changes were brought about by a few reformers, who realized that many people's working lives were unbearably hard. One great reformer was Anthony Ashley Cooper, the Earl of Shaftesbury (1801-85), who pushed many of the new laws through parliament.

Workers also learned to help themselves by joining trade unions and other societies. At first these were not accepted by politicians or employers, and even at the end of the Victorian age many workers did not have recognized rights.

► An official inspector talks to young girl workers during a factory visit in 1881. Inspectors questioned workers about their age and working conditions. In this case an overseer is listening and seems anxious to make a point. A reporter of the time wrote that most factory girls were well-behaved, intelligent and honest; the only problem was that, since most of them had worked since they were very small as well as going to school, they 'had little opportunity of learning household work'!

STRIKE!

ON THE

Taff Vale Railway.

Men's Headquarters,
Cobourn Street,
Cathays.

There has been a strike on the Taff Vale Railway since Monday last. The Management are using every means to decoy men here who they employ for the purpose of black-legging the men on strike.

Drivers, Firemen, Guards, Brakesmen, and SIGNALMEN, are all out.

Are you willing to be known as a

Blackleg?

If you accept employment on the Taff Vale, that is what you will be known by. On arriving at Cardiff, call at the above address, where you can get information and assistance.

RICHARD BELL,
General Secretary.

◀ *This **strike** poster was produced by the Amalgamated Society of Railway Servants in 1900. Workers who did not support the strike and went to work were known as **blacklegs**.*

▼ *The first successful national **trade union** was the Amalgamated Society of Engineers, which was formed in 1851. Various unions joined together to form the Trades Union Congress (TUC) in 1868. During the 1890s the trade union movement supported the formation of the Labour Party. This membership certificate dating from 1901 shows the two pillars of this particular workers' group: 'labour in unity; unity is strength'.*

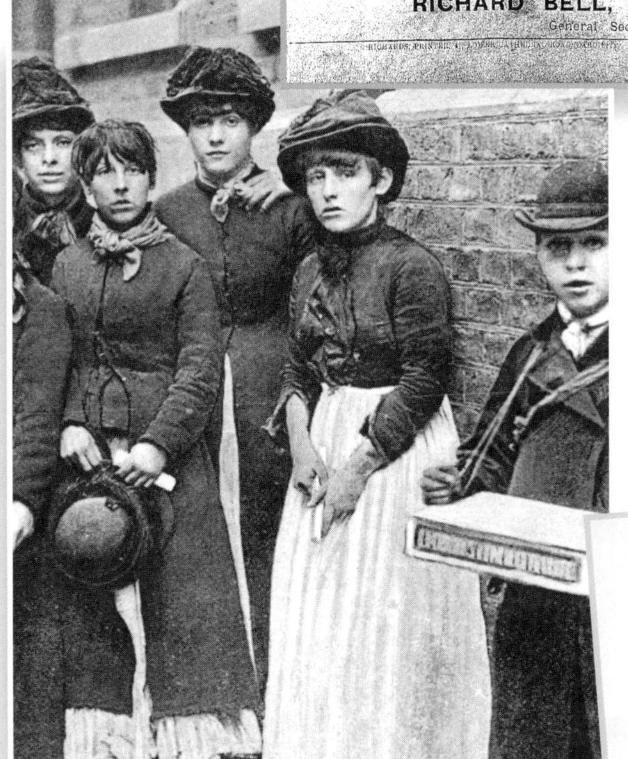

▲ *This photograph of 1888 shows London match girls out on strike. A visitor to the factory pointed out that the girls worked long hours in poor conditions. The factory manager tried to get the match girls to sign a document saying that they were well treated. When the girls refused, the manager sacked a girl he thought was their leader. All 1400 girls went on strike. Important people sided with the match girls, and finally the factory owner gave in and improved working conditions.*

FARMING

During Victorian times all British farmland was owned by the gentry, rich people with influence. The land was rented by farmers, who sometimes did quite well for themselves. And it was worked by farm labourers, who were generally paid very poorly.

When Victoria came to the throne, most people in Britain lived in the countryside and were involved in farming. During the second half of the nineteenth century, more and more people moved to the factory towns. Overall the population increased and this meant that more food was needed to feed the people. Farmers found ways of producing more food by using new machinery and discovering better ways of growing crops and rearing animals.

Farm work was very hard. Farm labourers had to work outdoors in all weathers, as ploughmen, shepherds and cowmen. Extra money could be earned at harvest time, when women often helped the men. Women generally also did the milking, and made butter and cheese in the dairy.

► *Farming methods continued to change in Victorian times. This farm machinery was new in the 1840s. From left to right, are a circular iron pig trough, a potato steamer, a wheelbarrow, a potato washer and a wrought iron feeding carriage.*

◄ *This 1843 illustration shows the special Christmas market at Smithfield, London, where farm-owners came to buy and sell cattle. In 1843 the cattle show was visited by Prince Albert. That year's Class 1 prize of £20 was won by Earl Spencer of Althorp, an ancestor of Princess Diana, for a fine Durham ox.*

◄ *This photograph was taken in 1887 and shows that old ploughing methods were still used. Most farmwork was done by hand. Here it is made to look peaceful and enjoyable, but it was hard work and poorly paid. Farmworkers changed jobs often. They looked for new positions and better wages by going to hiring fairs, which were held twice a year in most country towns. Farmers inspected the workers and decided which ones to take on.*

▼ *Steam engines made a big difference on larger farms, such as this one in 1851. Few farms could afford such equipment, so farmers hired it when they needed it. This steam engine is being used to power a large* ***flywheel****, which then turns the machinery in the thresher. In this way the grain was automatically separated from the corn, which saved time and labour. This steam engine won a prize from the Royal Agricultural Society.*

SHOPS

More people moved to the towns, and more shops opened to sell them the goods they needed. The shops also offered people jobs, such as serving customers and delivering goods, and sold goods made by manufacturers and craftsmen.

Village shops remained general stores, offering a wide range of goods. But in towns specialized shops grew in number. A typical row of shops might have a grocer selling food and household items, a butcher selling meat, a draper selling fabrics, a tailor selling clothes, a shoemaker and a barber. Costermongers sold fruit and vegetables from barrows in the street, and there might be other stallholders, selling fish, for example.

Co-operative stores were popular. The Co-operative Movement was inspired by the great reformer, Robert Owen (1771-1858), and was seen as a way of bringing shopkeepers and customers together. The first co-operative shop opened in Rochdale, Lancashire, in 1844. It sold quality goods at fair prices. Other people could join the Co-op, and at the end of each year profits were either shared out among the members or put back into the business.

► *Advertising grew rapidly in the second half of the nineteenth century, when newspapers and journals printed more and more ads. This example, dating from 1881, encouraged people to buy the ingredients for their plum pudding from the family grocers.*

► *Groceries were sold loose in Victorian shops, rather than in ready-made packages. This meant that each item had to be weighed and wrapped. Liquids were measured into bottles and jugs, and these were usually brought by the customers. This advertisement for new forms of packaging comes from 1901 and shows that times were starting to change. Today, many supermarkets are trying to use less packaging, to save energy and trees and create less rubbish.*

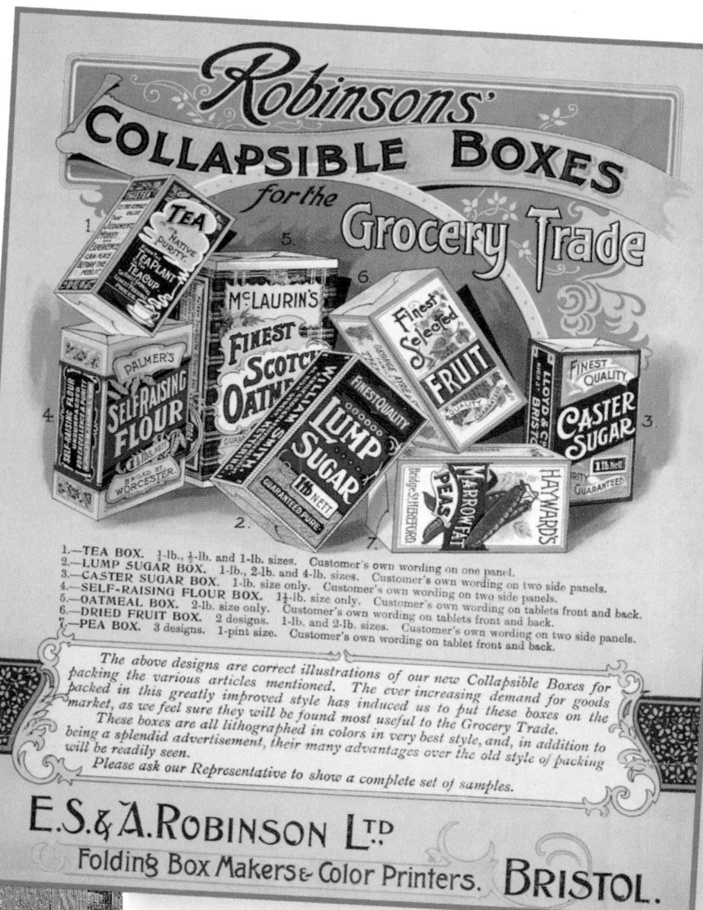

◄ *The shopping malls of the Victorian period were beautifully designed and decorated arcades. These illustrations show outside and inside a new arcade in Bond Street, London in 1880. The arcade contained 20 high-class shops.*

◄ *Three butchers and their dog stand proudly outside their shop in 1894. In those days people were not so concerned about standards of hygiene and didn't worry about the meat hanging outdoors. The sign above the shop says that the butchers are official purveyors, or suppliers, to Prince Arthur. He was the third son of Queen Victoria, and later became governor general of Canada.*

COMMUNICATION

Today you can send a message across the world in an instant in many different ways. Things were different in Victorian times, most news travelled slowly, by the printed word. Famous newspapers and journals such as *The Times, Observer* and *Tatler* were founded well before Victoria became queen. Others such as the *Daily Mail* (1896) began in the Victorian era.

The British postal system started in 1840, and the coming of the railways made it faster. By the 1860s several thousand kilometres of telegraph cables had been laid throughout Britain, which meant that people could send messages much more quickly. But the telegraph was used by very few, since it was expensive and there were not many telegraph offices.

Further developments such as the typewriter, first sold in America by Remington in 1874, and the telephone, which was invented in 1876 by Alexander Graham Bell, changed the world of communications. They also brought new forms of employment, especially to women.

► *Manufacturing a telegraph cable in 1851. This specially strong cable was made of four copper wires cased in* ***gutta-percha****, bound in* ***yarn*** *covered in tar, with an outer covering of ten iron wires. The manufacturing machine was powered by a steam engine and produced almost 5 metres of finished cable a minute. The total cable was almost 40 kilometres long and was laid on the floor of the English Channel between Dover and Calais, connecting Britain to France.*

▲ *This turn-of-the-century advertisement shows an early typewriter. By modern standards the early models were very heavy and cumbersome, but at the time they speeded up office work considerably. Women took to them more readily than men, and before long most secretaries were female. Official census reports show that in 1881 there were very few women clerks; by 1891 there were nearly 18 000 and by 1901 there were almost 56 000.*

▲ *This advertisement of 1897 shows that telephones and other electrical equipment were already available – to those who could afford them. The company also sold burglar alarms. The first public electricity was supplied by a power station at Godalming, Surrey, in 1881. But electricity did not become widely or cheaply available until after the Victorian age.*

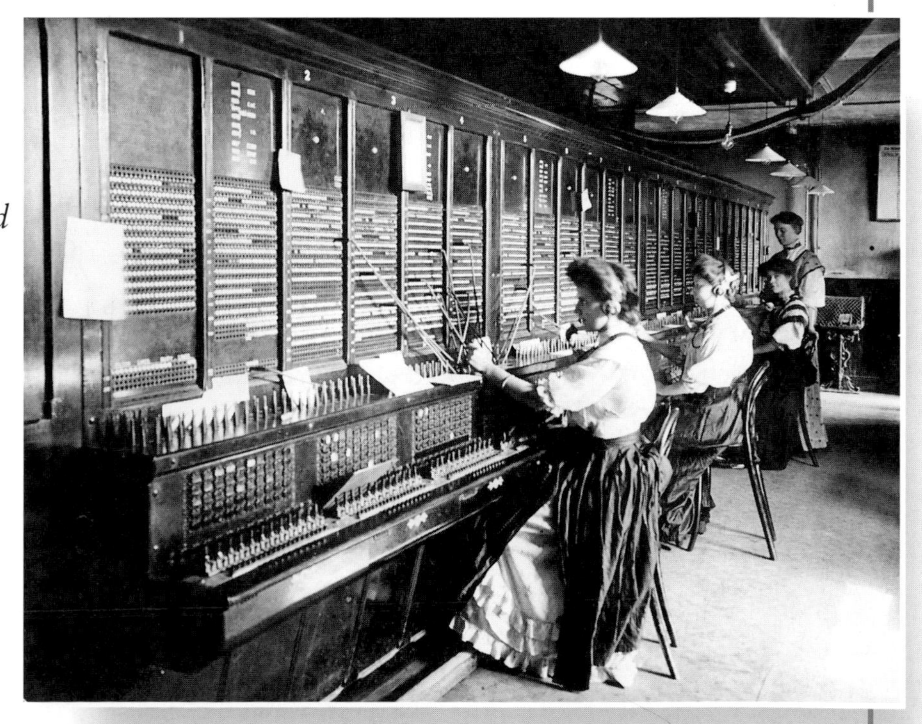

► *In a telephone exchange in 1900, each call was connected individually by an operator, who plugged connections into a* ***switchboard****. This could take quite a long time and sometimes failed altogether. Offices had manual switchboards until the 1960s, but today connections are made automatically or by electronic switching. Victorian telephone exchanges provided many jobs for women. By the end of the century almost half the workers in the telegraph and telephone service were female.*

Glossary

blackleg an insulting word for a worker who does not support a strike and goes on working.

butler the head man in charge of all the other male servants who also looked after the wine cellar and table cutlery.

calico a white fabric made from cotton.

cast iron iron which has been mixed with other materials and cast, or shaped, in a mould.

cog a wheel with teeth around the edge which can fit into another cog's teeth to turn it.

cottage industry a business that is carried out at home.

dormitory a large sleeping room with many beds.

exploit to take unfair advantage of people by not paying them what they deserve for the work they do.

flywheel a large, heavy wheel in a machine.

footman a uniformed male servant who opened doors in a house or carriage, helped to serve meals and carried messages.

forge to shape metal by beating and hammering it.

foundry a workshop where metal is cast.

governess a woman who is employed by the family to teach children at home.

gutta-percha a tough, rubbery substance that comes from Malaysian trees.

horsepower a measurement of power that was originally based on the pulling power of a strong horse.

housekeeper a woman whose job is to manage the household and who is in charge of all the other female servants.

import to buy and bring in from a foreign country.

industrial to do with industry and manufacturing things; industrial towns had many factories.

inmate a person who lives in an institution, such as a workhouse.

loom a machine for weaving thread into material.

nanny a woman who is employed by a family to look after young children.

nib the point of a pen.

nutritious food which is full of vitamins and minerals and which is good for your health.

orphan a child whose parents have died.

oversee to supervise, or watch, workers.

parish a local district.

patent to register an invention so that no-one else can copy it and sell it as their own.

pauper someone who had no money or belongings at all.

pollution the effects of smoke, waste and rubbish which make the air, land or water dirty.

quill a large feather which is sharpened so that it can be used as a pen.

rotary engine an engine that uses cogs and wheels to turn a driving belt and power machines.

spindle a thin rod in a spinning machine that is used for twisting and winding the thread.

strike when workers refuse to work as a protest against poor pay or conditions.

switchboard a board with electric sockets that can be plugged together to make telephone connections.

telegraph an electrical postal system which sent messages called telegrams across the country and overseas.

trade union an organization that looks after the rights and interests of a group of workers.

treadle a lever pushed back and forth by the operator's foot that makes a machine, such as a spinning wheel, work.

welfare help given to people in need, especially financial help.

workhouse a place where poor people received food and accommodation in return for work.

yarn spun thread used for weaving or knitting.

Index